THE DATA SCIENTIST'S MIND
Creativity Curiosity and Critical Thinking

Lateef Okunade

Copyright © 2024. All Rights Reserved.

The Data Scientist's Mind: Creativity Curiosity and Critical Thinking

Lateef Okunade

No part of this publication may be reproduced, distributed, or transmitted in any form or by any means, including photocopying, recording, or other electronic or mechanical methods, without prior written permission from the copyright owner.

This material is provided solely for educational and informational purposes and should not be considered financial advice.

The author and publisher do not endorse any commercial products or services linked to this book.

Globally Available

ISBN: 978-9-9911-0361-7

A catalogue record for this book is available at the National Library of Nigeria.

TABLE OF CONTENT

FOREWORD -- **iv**

INTRODUCTION ------------------------------------- **v**

CHAPTER 1: INTRODUCTION TO THE DATA SCIENTIST'S MIND. ---- **1**

CHAPTER 2: THE FOUNDATION OF CRITICAL THINKING IN DATA SCIENCE. -- **9**

CHAPTER 3: CURIOSITY AS THE CATALYST FOR DATA DISCOVERY -- **19**

CHAPTER 4: CREATIVITY IN DATA SCIENCE: BEYOND THE ALGORITHMS -- **25**

CHAPTER 5: BLENDING CREATIVITY AND CRITICAL THINKING IN PROBLEM SOLVING. -- **33**

CHAPTER 6: ASKING THE RIGHT QUESTIONS: THE CORE OF DATA SCIENCE -- **39**

CHAPTER 7: THE ART OF DATA STORYTELLING -------------- **47**

CHAPTER 8: TACKLING AMBIGUITY: NAVIGATING UNCERTAINTY IN DATA -- **55**

CHAPTER 9: THE BALANCE OF INTUITION AND DATA ---------- **63**

CHAPTER 10: THE HOLISTIC DATA SCIENTIST: INTEGRATING CREATIVITY, CURIOSITY, CRITICAL THINKING, AND INTUITION. -- **71**

FOREWORD

In today's data-driven world, the role of a data scientist has evolved beyond just crunching numbers and running algorithms. It now requires a blend of creativity, curiosity, and critical thinking—a unique combination that enables professionals to not only solve complex problems but to envision possibilities where others see only data. This book, **The Data Scientist's Mind**, captures that essence. The power of data is undeniable, but the true value of a data scientist lies in their ability to transform raw information into meaningful insights. This book takes you on a journey through the mental processes that shape the best data-driven decisions, exploring how curiosity sparks the exploration of data, how creativity unlocks innovative solutions, and how critical thinking ensures precision and accuracy. As you delve into the chapters ahead, you will discover that the heart of data science is not merely about technical proficiency but about the mindset that drives it. The thoughtful exploration of these essential qualities provides a fresh perspective on the data science profession. By highlighting real-world examples and actionable strategies, this book challenges readers to expand their own thinking and approach data science not as a rigid field but as one that thrives on intellectual flexibility and imagination. Whether you are an aspiring data scientist or a seasoned expert, this book offers valuable insights that will reshape how you approach your work. I am confident that, by the end of this journey, you will have a renewed appreciation for the boundless opportunities that lie at the intersection of creativity, curiosity, and critical thinking.

Let this book inspire you to think beyond the data.

INTRODUCTION

The field of data science has exploded in recent years, becoming one of the most sought-after and influential professions across industries. Businesses, governments, and organizations are turning to data scientists to help them make informed decisions, optimize processes, and predict future trends. From financial institutions seeking to detect fraud to healthcare providers aiming to improve patient outcomes, the power of data science is transforming the way we operate, plan, and solve problems. Yet, despite its technical foundations, the true power of data science lies in the mind of the person handling the data. This book takes a deep dive into the often-overlooked traits that make data scientists not just competent, but exceptional: creativity, curiosity, and critical thinking. While many people associate data science with numbers, algorithms, and vast data sets, it is, at its core, a human endeavor. Data itself is neutral—meaningless until it is interpreted, analyzed, and applied to real-world problems. The value of data science stems not from the data alone but from how it is harnessed, processed, and turned into actionable insights.

This transformation doesn't happen through technical proficiency alone; it requires a specific mindset—a combination of curiosity, creativity, and critical thinking—that allows data scientists to move beyond the data and into the realm of innovation. At its heart, data science is about curiosity. Every data scientist starts with a question—a desire to explore the unknown and uncover patterns that others may not see. This relentless curiosity is what drives the field forward, pushing data scientists to ask "why" and "what if" at every turn. A curious mind doesn't accept things at face value; it probes deeper, eager to discover the hidden connections and possibilities within the data. Curiosity is the spark that sets the entire data science process in motion, and it is this innate desire to explore and understand that separates average data professionals from exceptional ones. But curiosity alone is not enough to navigate the complex landscape of data science. Enter creativity. The problems faced by data scientists are often multifaceted and ambiguous, with no clear-cut solutions.

In these situations, creativity becomes essential. It is the creative mind that imagines new ways to model data, visualizes fresh ways to present insights, and devises innovative algorithms to handle unstructured or incomplete information. Creativity in data science doesn't always mean thinking outside the box—it often means building a better box altogether. The ability to think creatively is what allows data scientists to adapt to new challenges, innovate solutions, and apply their technical knowledge in ways that haven't been done before. Critical thinking is the glue that binds curiosity and creativity together. It is the framework that ensures that the questions data scientists ask and the solutions they propose are grounded in logic, evidence, and accuracy. In the modern data landscape, where information is abundant and often overwhelming, the ability to critically assess data sources, interpret results, and draw valid conclusions is more important than ever. Critical thinking provides the rigor needed to filter through the noise, avoid biases, and make data-driven decisions that are reliable and actionable.

Without this essential trait, even the most creative and curious data scientist runs the risk of being misled by incomplete or inaccurate data. Together, creativity, curiosity, and critical thinking form the trifecta of traits that define the data scientist's mind. These traits allow data scientists to explore new frontiers, devise novel solutions, and draw insights that go beyond surface-level observations. But how can we develop and nurture these qualities in ourselves or our teams? How can we train our minds to think beyond the data and see the bigger picture? This book will explore those questions, offering practical strategies for cultivating a mindset that not only thrives in data science but excels at it. In the chapters that follow, we will explore how these three traits manifest in different stages of the data science process. We will examine the role of curiosity in framing the right questions and how creativity can help overcome common challenges like incomplete data or noisy signals. We will delve into the importance of critical thinking in verifying the validity of insights and how these traits come together to create truly impactful data-driven solutions.

This book is not just a guide for those new to data science; it's also an invitation for experienced data professionals to reflect on their approach and consider how they might enhance their work by focusing on the human aspects of data science. One of the most exciting aspects of data science is that it is constantly evolving. As new technologies, methods, and tools emerge, the field continues to expand into areas that were previously unimaginable. Yet, amidst all these advancements, the human mind remains the most powerful tool of all. The ability to approach data with a creative, curious, and critical mindset will always be the most valuable asset a data scientist can possess. This is especially true as we move into an era where artificial intelligence and automation are becoming more prevalent in data science workflows. While machines can process data faster and more efficiently than ever before, they lack the human traits that drive innovation, exploration, and ethical decision-making. As you read this book, I encourage you to think of it not just as a guide but as a conversation about what it means to be a data scientist in today's world.

Consider the role your curiosity plays in your work. Reflect on how creativity has helped you solve a particularly tough problem or uncover an unexpected insight. And, most importantly, think about how critical thinking underpins everything you do, ensuring that your conclusions are sound, and your decisions are based on more than just intuition. These traits—creativity, curiosity, and critical thinking—are not just important; they are essential to thriving in this ever-changing field. Data science is not just a discipline of numbers and models; it is a journey of discovery, fueled by the same qualities that have driven human progress for centuries. Whether you are just starting your journey or are well along the path, this book will serve as a reminder that, at the end of the day, the most important tool in data science isn't the algorithm—it's the mind behind it.

"The important thing is not to stop questioning. Curiosity has its own reason for existing." — Albert Einstein

"Creativity is intelligence having fun." — Albert Einstein

"Critical thinking is the key to creative problem-solving in business." — Richard Branson

CHAPTER 1

INTRODUCTION TO THE DATA SCIENTIST'S MIND.

At first glance, data science may seem like it's all about numbers, equations, and algorithms. It's easy to fall into the assumption that the most important skills a data scientist needs are purely technical, like knowing how to program in Python or R, mastering statistical analysis, or understanding machine learning algorithms. These are indeed critical components of the job. Without technical proficiency, it's difficult to even begin tackling the problems data scientists are hired to solve. However, focusing solely on technical skills tells only part of the story. In reality, data science is much more than simply applying mathematical formulas or running machine learning models. The technical aspects form the foundation, but they are just that: the starting point. What truly sets successful data scientists apart is their mindset—their ability to think creatively, ask the right questions, and analyze data critically. In a rapidly evolving field like data science, where the tools and technologies change constantly, it's the mindset of a data scientist that becomes the most valuable asset.

Let's take an example: two data scientists are tasked with predicting customer churn for a company. Both have access to the same tools, the same data, and the same algorithms. One might approach the problem as purely a technical exercise, running models to see what works, tweaking parameters, and optimizing the final result. The other might start by questioning the data itself, examining patterns, thinking creatively about potential external factors that might influence churn, and critically assessing the quality and completeness of the data set. This second data scientist isn't just applying tools; they're thinking deeply about the problem, being curious about what might lie beyond the data they've been given and using critical thinking to question every assumption. As a result, the second data scientist is far more likely to uncover insights that will make a real difference to the business. The world of data science is often messy and ambiguous. The problems data scientists face rarely come with clear instructions or obvious solutions.

For example, datasets are often incomplete, noisy, or full of biases. Sometimes, the data you have doesn't answer the questions you need to solve, requiring you to explore external sources or approach the problem from a different angle. This is where creativity comes into play, being able to navigate these challenges and still find innovative ways to extract value from the data. A creative data scientist can transform limitations into opportunities, turning incomplete datasets into gold mines of insight. Curiosity, too, is an essential trait. Data science is driven by exploration and discovery. A data scientist who approaches their work with genuine curiosity is more likely to uncover patterns and insights that others miss. They don't just accept things at face value; they dig deeper, constantly asking "Why?" and "What if?" They experiment, test, and explore all possible angles before arriving at conclusions. Curiosity drives the data scientist to explore not just the obvious patterns but also the anomalies—the unusual outliers in the data that can sometimes lead to groundbreaking insights.

However, creativity and curiosity must be balanced by critical thinking. In a field where data-driven decisions impact everything from business strategy to public health, it's crucial that data scientists evaluate their results with a sharp, analytical mind. They must constantly question the validity of their assumptions, verify the quality of their data, and scrutinize the conclusions they draw. Critical thinking ensures that creativity and curiosity don't lead down the wrong path. It helps data scientists avoid common pitfalls such as overfitting models, falling for misleading correlations, or making decisions based on incomplete information. In short, while technical skills are the foundation of data science, they are only the beginning. What truly elevates a data scientist's work is their ability to combine creativity, curiosity, and critical thinking. This chapter sets the stage by exploring how these three traits shape the mindset of a successful data scientist and how they are applied in practice. Throughout the rest of this book, we will examine how creativity, curiosity, and critical thinking can be cultivated and harnessed to solve complex data problems, uncover hidden insights, and ultimately, drive impactful results.

The Evolution of Data Science

Data science has grown from its roots in statistics and computer science into a field that influences nearly every industry. Today, data scientists are employed in finance, healthcare, retail, government, and beyond, tasked with turning vast amounts of data into actionable insights. However, as the field has expanded, so too have the challenges. Gone are the days when simple statistical models were enough to answer business questions. Today, data scientists are expected to solve complex, multifaceted problems that often have no clear solutions. In this environment, technical proficiency is not enough. A data scientist needs to be able to navigate ambiguity, find patterns where others see noise, and communicate complex ideas to non-technical stakeholders. These challenges require more than just knowledge of algorithms—they demand a different way of thinking, one that balances the technical with the creative, and the analytical with the imaginative.

The Power of Creativity in Data Science

One of the most surprising aspects of data science is the need for creativity. Creativity is not typically associated with fields like mathematics or statistics, yet it is essential for problem-solving in data science. Why? Because real-world data is messy, incomplete, and often presents more questions than answers. Data scientists must use their creativity to design models, craft visualizations, and develop solutions that address unique and often novel problems. For instance, imagine you are tasked with building a predictive model for customer behavior, but you have limited data on hand. The traditional approach might not work because of the data limitations. A creative data scientist will think outside the box—perhaps by incorporating external data sources, applying novel data augmentation techniques, or re-framing the problem in a way that makes it more manageable. Creativity in data science is not just about coming up with clever solutions. It's also about being able to visualize data in ways that make the insights clear to others. A well-designed data visualization can tell a story, communicate a complex insight in a simple way, and inspire decision-makers to take action. In this sense, data scientists are part artist, tasked with crafting visual stories from numbers and trends.

Curiosity: The Driving Force Behind Discovery

If creativity helps a data scientist solve problems, then curiosity is what gets them started. The best data scientists are naturally curious. They don't just accept data at face value; they are constantly asking questions, digging deeper, and exploring what lies beneath the surface. This curiosity is essential because data science is not just about answering questions, it's about asking the right ones. Data scientists deal with enormous amounts of data, much of which might seem irrelevant or overwhelming at first glance. But a curious data scientist is always wondering, "What patterns am I not seeing?" or "What does this anomaly mean?" It is through this relentless questioning that new insights emerge. Curiosity leads to exploration, and exploration leads to discovery. Curiosity also drives experimentation. In data science, not every approach works the first time. It requires a willingness to try different methods, to test hypotheses, and to iterate on models. The curious mind does not shy away from failed attempts or dead ends; instead, it sees them as learning opportunities. This mindset is what leads to breakthroughs in data science.

Critical Thinking: The Foundation of Data-Driven Decisions

While creativity and curiosity are essential, they must be balanced with critical thinking. Data science, after all, is about making informed, data-driven decisions. Critical thinking ensures that creativity and curiosity don't lead you down the wrong path. It is the filter through which ideas must pass before they are turned into action. Critical thinking in data science involves skepticism, evaluation, and reflection. Data scientists must always be skeptical of their data—asking questions like, "Is this data reliable?" and "What biases might be influencing the results?" Critical thinkers don't just accept the first result they get; they scrutinize it, look for alternative explanations, and test their assumptions. Data can be misleading, and without strong critical thinking skills, it's easy to draw incorrect conclusions. For example, correlation does not imply causation, and data sets often have hidden biases that can skew results. A data scientist who is not thinking critically may fall into these traps, producing results that seem valid on the surface but are ultimately flawed. Moreover, critical thinking is essential for communicating data insights. Data scientists often work with non-technical stakeholders, executives, clients, or business teams—who may not understand the complexities of data science. Critical thinking helps data scientists present their findings in a clear, logical, and concise manner, making sure the insights are grounded in evidence and are actionable.

The Data Scientist's Mindset: A Holistic Approach

So, what does it mean to have the "mind of a data scientist"? It means embracing a mindset that combines creativity, curiosity, and critical thinking in equal measure. A creative mind sees possibilities where others see limitations. A curious mind drives exploration and discovery, always pushing the boundaries of what data can tell us. And a critical mind ensures that every decision is based on solid evidence and sound logic. In the chapters that follow, we will delve deeper into each of these traits—how they shape the data science process, how they can be nurtured, and how they interact to produce innovative solutions. Whether you're new to data science or a seasoned professional, this book will offer fresh insights into how you can elevate your work by focusing on the mindset that drives the field. Data science is not just a technical discipline; it is a way of thinking. By cultivating the traits of creativity, curiosity, and critical thinking, you can unlock new possibilities, solve complex problems, and create lasting impact through your work.

LATEEF OKUNADE

CHAPTER 2

THE FOUNDATION OF CRITICAL THINKING IN DATA SCIENCE.

In the world of data science, where decisions are data-driven and evidence-based, critical thinking is the foundation that ensures the accuracy, relevance, and reliability of insights. Unlike fields where intuition or gut feelings may guide decision-making, data science relies heavily on a systematic approach to interpreting information. Data-driven decisions have a significant impact on everything from business strategies to medical diagnostics, and as such, they must be grounded in a rigorous process that carefully evaluates all available data. This is where critical thinking comes into play. Critical thinking in data science involves a continuous process of analyzing, interpreting, evaluating, and synthesizing information from multiple sources to form a well-reasoned judgment. It is not merely about applying technical skills like running statistical models or creating machine learning algorithms. Instead, it's about thinking deeply and independently about the data you are working with.

A Data Scientist must constantly ask themselves: ***"What assumptions am I making? Is this data reliable? Could there be alternative explanations for these results?"*** For instance, let's consider a scenario in which a company is experiencing a decline in sales, and a data scientist is tasked with finding out why. Without critical thinking, they may quickly conclude that the sales drop is due to a seasonal slump or a temporary market downturn. However, a critical thinker will dig deeper. They will look for hidden variables, examine trends over multiple time frames, and consider other potential factors such as customer satisfaction, product quality, or even the impact of competitors. This deeper analysis is what separates a mere technician from a true data scientist. A critical thinking mindset helps to avoid common cognitive biases that can skew the interpretation of data. For example, confirmation bias—a tendency to favor information that confirms existing beliefs—can lead a data scientist to overemphasize findings that support their initial hypothesis while ignoring data that contradicts it. A critical thinker will actively guard against this bias, seeking out alternative perspectives and questioning their assumptions to ensure that the analysis is objective and comprehensive.

Moreover, data is often messy, incomplete, or inconsistent, requiring data scientists to make decisions about how to handle these imperfections. Critical thinking ensures that these decisions are thoughtful and evidence-based rather than arbitrary. When encountering missing data, for example, a critical thinker will ask whether it's better to impute the missing values, remove the incomplete records, or adjust the model in some other way. They will weigh the consequences of each option and choose the one that has the least potential for introducing bias or inaccuracies. In essence, critical thinking serves as a safeguard against errors, biases, and flawed conclusions. It enables data scientists to not only process data but to understand its limitations and extract meaningful insights that can guide decision-making. This disciplined approach ensures that conclusions drawn from data are not only accurate but also actionable and reliable. As we explore the role of critical thinking in more detail throughout this chapter, we will see how it influences every stage of the data process, from problem definition to data collection, analysis, and communication of results. Ultimately, critical thinking is what allows data scientists to turn raw data into valuable insights that can drive impactful, data-driven decisions.

What is Critical Thinking?

At its core, critical thinking is the ability to think clearly and rationally, understanding the logical connections between ideas. It is a form of reflective and independent thinking, in which one carefully considers the relevance, accuracy, and significance of information before drawing conclusions. Critical thinking is not about memorizing facts or following procedures blindly, it's about questioning information, identifying underlying assumptions, evaluating evidence, and approaching problems from multiple perspectives. In data science, critical thinking plays an essential role because data often presents more questions than answers. Data scientists are tasked with making sense of large, complex datasets and translating that information into actionable insights. Without a strong foundation of critical thinking, even the most sophisticated algorithms or models can lead to inaccurate conclusions, poor decision-making, and costly errors.

The Role of Critical Thinking in Data Science

Critical thinking permeates every step of the data science process, from the initial stages of data collection and cleaning to the final stages of model deployment and decision-making. Below are the key areas where critical thinking is essential in data science.

1. Defining the Problem

The first stage of any data science project is defining the problem. This might seem straightforward, but often it requires deep critical thinking to frame the problem correctly. In data science, asking the right question is half the battle. A poorly defined problem will lead to poor results, no matter how sophisticated the analysis or model is. Critical thinking helps data scientists move beyond surface-level questions to uncover the root of the issue. For example, a business might approach a data scientist with the question, "How can we increase sales?" While this question seems clear, it is vague and open to multiple interpretations. A critical thinker will break down the question: Are we talking about short-term or long-term sales? Which product lines are the focus? Should we look at customer behavior, marketing strategies, or pricing models? By digging deeper and refining the question, a data scientist can ensure they are addressing the right problem, setting the stage for a more effective analysis.

2. Data Collection and Validation

Once the problem is clearly defined, the next step is to collect and validate the data. At this stage, critical thinking is vital for evaluating the quality and reliability of the data. Data scientists need to ask critical questions such as: Is the data accurate? Is it complete? Are there any biases in the data? Where does the data come from? Are the sources trustworthy? Without this scrutiny, a data scientist might unknowingly base their analysis on flawed or incomplete data, leading to unreliable results. Data validation is an ongoing process throughout the data science pipeline, and critical thinking ensures that data scientists continuously question the quality of the data they are working with. For instance, a dataset might contain outliers or missing values. Rather than dismissing these anomalies, a critical thinker will investigate further: Are these outliers errors, or do they represent a significant trend that needs attention? Could the missing data impact the analysis, or is it negligible? This type of critical analysis allows data scientists to make informed decisions about how to handle data quality issues.

3. Data Exploration and Analysis

Data exploration is one of the most creative and exciting parts of data science, but it also requires a critical mind. During data exploration, data scientists seek to uncover patterns, trends, and relationships within the data. While visualization tools and statistical methods help in this process, critical thinking enables data scientists to ask meaningful questions about the data: What do these patterns mean? Are they real, or could they be due to random chance? Could other factors explain these trends? One of the most significant pitfalls in data analysis is mistaking correlation for causation. Just because two variables are correlated doesn't mean that one causes the other. A classic example of this is the correlation between ice cream sales and drowning incidents, while both increase during the summer months, one does not cause the other. Without critical thinking, it's easy to jump to conclusions based on correlations alone. A good data scientist knows to ask: What other variables might be at play? Could there be a third factor influencing both variables?

4. Hypothesis Testing and Model Building

In many data science projects, data scientists must develop and test hypotheses. This involves proposing a potential explanation for a phenomenon and then using data to test whether that explanation holds. Critical thinking is essential in this process because it helps data scientists remain objective and skeptical of their own assumptions. A good hypothesis is one that is testable and falsifiable, meaning that it can be proven wrong. A data scientist must be open to the possibility that their hypothesis is incorrect and willing to revise it in light of new evidence. Similarly, when building models, critical thinking helps data scientists evaluate whether the model is appropriate for the problem at hand. For example, should you use a linear regression model or a decision tree? Is the model overfitting or underfitting the data? What assumptions does the model make, and are those assumptions reasonable in this context? A critical thinker will carefully consider these questions, ensuring that the model is not only accurate but also interpretable and robust.

5. Interpretation of Results

Perhaps the most crucial stage where critical thinking comes into play is in interpreting the results of a data analysis or model. At this stage, the data scientist must carefully examine the outcomes, looking for possible sources of error or bias. Just because a model produces a high accuracy score doesn't mean the results are reliable. Critical thinkers must evaluate whether the model's predictions are meaningful and whether they align with real-world expectations. Bias is a particularly significant issue in data interpretation. Data scientists must be aware of both algorithmic and human biases that can creep into the analysis. For example, if a model is trained on biased data, it will likely produce biased predictions. Critical thinkers will question the sources of bias and take steps to mitigate them, ensuring that the results are fair, accurate, and actionable.

6. Decision-Making and Communication

Finally, critical thinking is essential when it comes to decision-making and communicating the findings of a data science project. Data scientists often work closely with business leaders, executives, and other stakeholders who may not have a deep understanding of the technical aspects of the analysis. It's the data scientist's job to present the findings in a way that is clear, concise, and actionable. Critical thinking helps data scientists distill complex analyses into insights that decision-makers can understand. It also ensures that data scientists consider the broader implications of their findings. For example, if a model predicts that certain customers are likely to churn, a critical thinker will not only present that result but also consider the impact of various interventions, weighing the costs and benefits of each approach. This holistic thinking leads to better, more informed decision-making.

Developing Critical Thinking Skills as a Data Scientist

Now that we've explored the importance of critical thinking in data science, the question remains: How can one develop and strengthen these skills? Below are a few strategies for cultivating a critical thinking mindset in data science.

1. Practice Skepticism: One of the key components of critical thinking is skepticism. Data scientists should always question their assumptions, data sources, and conclusions. By practicing skepticism, you can avoid taking information at face value and develop a deeper understanding of the problem at hand. Ask yourself: Is this data accurate? Are these results too good to be true? What biases might be influencing my conclusions?

2. Embrace Complexity: Critical thinking involves being comfortable with complexity and ambiguity. Data science problems are rarely black and white, and there are often multiple variables and factors at play. Embrace the complexity of the problems you face and be open to considering multiple explanations and solutions. This flexibility will allow you to approach problems from different angles and find creative solutions.

3. Engage in Continuous Learning: Critical thinking is a skill that improves with practice. By continually learning about new techniques, methods, and tools in data science, you can strengthen your ability to think critically about your work. Stay curious and engaged in the field, attending conferences, reading papers, and engaging in discussions with peers. The more knowledge you have, the better equipped you will be to think critically about the data science problems you encounter.

4. Collaborate and Seek Feedback: Collaboration is another way to develop critical thinking skills. Working with others allows you to hear different perspectives and challenge your own assumptions. Seek feedback from your peers and mentors and be open to constructive criticism. By engaging in dialogue with others, you can refine your thinking and approach problems with a more well-rounded perspective.

Critical thinking is the foundation upon which data science rests. It is what allows data scientists to move beyond surface-level observations, identify meaningful patterns, and make informed decisions that drive real impact. Whether it's in defining the problem, evaluating data quality, analyzing trends, or communicating results, critical thinking ensures that data science is not just a technical exercise but a rigorous, thoughtful process. As we continue through this book, you will see how critical thinking interacts with creativity and curiosity, forming the three pillars of the data scientist's mind. Together, these traits enable data scientists to not only solve problems but to push the boundaries of what is possible with data.

LATEEF OKUNADE

CHAPTER 3

CURIOSITY AS THE CATALYST FOR DATA DISCOVERY

If critical thinking forms the backbone of a data scientist's mindset, curiosity is the force that propels the journey forward. In data science, curiosity is more than just an innate sense of wonder; it's an essential trait that drives the exploration of data, the formulation of new questions, and the relentless pursuit of insights. Without curiosity, data science would be reduced to a rote, mechanical process. But curiosity ignites a passion for discovery, leading data scientists to push boundaries, explore unconventional paths, and uncover hidden patterns that might otherwise remain buried in the data. Curiosity is the catalyst for innovation in data science. It drives the data scientist to ask, "Why is this happening?" or "What if we approached this problem differently?" This desire to learn and understand is the starting point for any meaningful exploration of data. In this chapter, we will explore the role of curiosity in data science, how it leads to more effective data exploration, and why it is critical in developing insights that truly make a difference.

The Nature of Curiosity in Data Science

Curiosity, at its core, is the urge to explore the unknown. For a data scientist, this often means diving into vast amounts of data without fully knowing what they might find. In the initial stages of a project, there may be only a vague idea of the patterns, trends, or relationships that exist in the data. Curiosity is what drives the data scientist to explore further, to test hypotheses, and to experiment with different approaches. A curious data scientist does not settle for surface-level insights. Instead, they probe deeper, continuously asking questions like, "What is causing this anomaly?" or "How do these two variables interact in ways that we didn't expect?" This mindset prevents data scientists from taking the data at face value, encouraging them to investigate beyond the obvious and to explore avenues others might overlook. Moreover, curiosity fosters resilience. Not every data exploration leads to groundbreaking insights, and many paths turn out to be dead ends. But a curious data scientist does not view these dead ends as failures. Instead, they see them as learning opportunities that provide valuable information about the data and the problem at hand. In this way, curiosity breeds persistence—an essential trait for working through the complexity and ambiguity that often characterizes real-world data problems.

Curiosity as a Tool for Asking the Right Questions

One of the most valuable contributions of curiosity to data science is the ability to ask better, more insightful questions. Data science is often driven by questions: What problem are we trying to solve? What data do we need? What insights will be useful to stakeholders? The quality of the questions asked at the outset of a project often determines the quality of the final insights. Curiosity plays a crucial role in shaping these questions. When a data scientist approaches a dataset with a curious mindset, they are more likely to ask open-ended, exploratory questions that go beyond the obvious. Instead of focusing solely on confirming known trends or validating existing theories, a curious data scientist will look for patterns and relationships that have not yet been considered. This approach can lead to unexpected insights and new ways of thinking about the problem. For example, in the context of customer behavior, a curious data scientist might not only ask, "Which customers are likely to churn?" but also, "What early behaviors signal a shift in customer loyalty?" or "What unexpected factors might influence customer decisions?" These questions go beyond the immediate need and delve into deeper, more nuanced aspects of the problem, paving the way for innovative solutions. The process of asking the right questions is iterative, and curiosity drives this iteration. A data scientist with a curious mindset constantly refines their questions as they learn more about the data. Each discovery leads to new questions, creating a feedback loop that fuels further exploration and analysis.

Exploring the Unknown: Curiosity in Data Exploration

Data exploration is one of the most exciting parts of data science, and curiosity is its driving force. In this phase, data scientists begin with an open mind, looking for patterns, correlations, anomalies, or any signals in the data that might point them in the right direction. It's in this phase that curiosity truly comes alive, as the data scientist navigates through a sea of information, unsure of what they will find but eager to discover. Curiosity allows data scientists to embrace uncertainty. Unlike some fields where the outcome is known from the start, data exploration is often a journey into the unknown. There is no guaranteed path to success, and it's impossible to know in advance whether a particular line of inquiry will yield valuable insights. But a curious data scientist approaches this uncertainty with excitement rather than hesitation. They understand that the process of exploration is valuable in itself, even if it doesn't lead to immediate breakthroughs. Curiosity also encourages data scientists to explore unconventional or less obvious patterns.

In many cases, the most valuable insights come not from the obvious relationships in the data, but from the unexpected ones. A curious data scientist is willing to experiment with different approaches, whether that's applying a new algorithm, testing a different visualization, or looking at the data from an unusual angle. This experimentation is often the key to uncovering insights that others might miss. For instance, imagine a scenario where a company is analyzing customer data to improve its marketing strategy. While most data scientists might focus on obvious metrics like purchase history or customer demographics, a curious data scientist might take a different approach. They might explore patterns in the timing of purchases, social media interactions, or customer support inquiries. This broader exploration could lead to surprising insights—perhaps customers who frequently contact support are more likely to make repeat purchases, or customers who interact with certain marketing content at specific times are more likely to convert. Without curiosity, these hidden relationships might never come to light.

Curiosity and Continuous Learning

Another vital aspect of curiosity in data science is its role in fostering continuous learning. The field of data science is constantly evolving, with new techniques, tools, and methodologies emerging regularly. A curious data scientist is naturally inclined to stay up to date with the latest developments, eager to learn new skills and apply them to their work. Curiosity pushes data scientists to explore new technologies and methodologies, even when they are outside their immediate area of expertise. For example, a data scientist with a background in statistical modeling might be curious about machine learning techniques or deep learning algorithms. This curiosity can lead them to experiment with new tools, broadening their skillset and improving their ability to solve complex problems. Furthermore, a curious data scientist is open to learning from failure. Not every experiment will succeed, and not every hypothesis will be correct. But rather than being discouraged by setbacks, a curious data scientist views them as opportunities to learn. They ask themselves, "What can I learn from this failure?" and use that knowledge to improve their approach in the future. In this way, curiosity not only drives the exploration of data but also fosters personal and professional growth. It keeps data scientists engaged with their field, encourages them to take risks, and pushes them to continuously refine their skills and methods.

Curiosity's Role in Driving Innovation

Innovation in data science often stems from a willingness to explore uncharted territory, to ask questions that others haven't thought of yet, and to experiment with new ideas and approaches. This is where curiosity plays a critical role. Many groundbreaking advancements in data science have come from curious individuals who were willing to challenge the status quo. For instance, the development of recommendation systems—algorithms that predict what users might like based on their past behavior—came from curious minds who asked, "How can we use data to personalize the user experience in a meaningful way?" These data scientists didn't stop analyzing user behavior on a surface level; they sought deeper patterns and created algorithms that have since become a cornerstone of modern e-commerce, entertainment, and social media platforms. Similarly, the development of artificial intelligence and machine learning algorithms has been driven by the curiosity to understand and replicate human intelligence. Curiosity has pushed data scientists and researchers to experiment with different neural network architectures, leading to breakthroughs in natural language processing, image recognition, and autonomous systems.

In day-to-day data science practice, curiosity leads to small but impactful innovations. It might inspire a data scientist to test a new feature engineering technique, explore an alternative visualization method, or apply an unconventional algorithm to a problem. Each of these small acts of curiosity contributes to the ongoing evolution of data science as a field. Curiosity is the engine that drives data discovery. It fuels the desire to explore the unknown, ask better questions, and continuously learn from both success and failure. A curious data scientist doesn't settle for surface-level insights but digs deeper, relentlessly seeking new patterns and relationships within the data. This mindset of exploration and discovery is what leads to true innovation in data science, allowing professionals to uncover insights that can transform industries and solve complex problems. As we move forward, we will see how curiosity interacts with critical thinking and creativity to create a holistic approach to problem-solving in data science. Together, these traits form the foundation of the data scientist's mind, enabling them to not only analyze data but also push the boundaries of what's possible with it.

CHAPTER 4

CREATIVITY IN DATA SCIENCE: BEYOND THE ALGORITHMS

In data science, creativity is often considered the secret ingredient that separates an average data scientist from an exceptional one. While the field is deeply rooted in mathematics, programming, and statistical models, it is also a discipline that demands innovative thinking and creative problem-solving. Creativity in data science transcends the traditional boundaries of algorithms and coding; it's about the ability to approach problems with fresh perspectives, to envision new possibilities, and to craft unique solutions to complex challenges. At first glance, data science might seem to be a purely technical field, dominated by rules, procedures, and structured methodologies. After all, data science deals heavily with numbers, logical reasoning, and quantitative analysis. However, data is often messy, ambiguous, and incomplete, and standard methods don't always yield the answers you need. This is where creativity becomes cruciality, allowing a data scientist to navigate these challenges, think outside the box, and devise solutions that standard approaches might not offer.

One of the most significant aspects of creativity in data science is the ability to ask the right questions. While technical skills can help a data scientist process large datasets and build models, creativity helps them step back and consider the broader picture: What questions should we be asking? Are we looking at the right metrics? How can we approach this problem in a way that others might not have considered? Often, the most valuable insights arise not from advanced algorithms but from asking the right questions in the first place. Creativity enables data scientists to dig deeper and go beyond surface-level patterns, allowing them to explore alternative explanations and potential insights that may have otherwise been overlooked. Creativity also plays a key role in data preprocessing and feature engineering, the process of preparing raw data for modelling by transforming it into meaningful features.

When data is incomplete or noisy, a creative data scientist will devise methods to handle missing information, identify outliers, and create new features that better capture the underlying patterns in the data. For example, instead of using straightforward variables like age or income, a creative data scientist might combine variables to create new features, such as "customer engagement score" or "lifetime value index," to more accurately represent customer behavior. These creative transformations can significantly improve model performance and lead to deeper insights. Moreover, creativity is essential when it comes to visualizing data and presenting findings to stakeholders. Communicating insights from data is as much about storytelling as it is about analysis. A creative data scientist knows how to turn complex datasets into clear, engaging, and visually compelling stories. Rather than overwhelming the audience with technical jargon or endless rows of numbers, creative data visualizations can simplify the data, highlight key trends, and make the information digestible for non-experts.

Whether it's through interactive dashboards, custom visualizations, or creative use of colors and shapes, a well-crafted visualization can make all the difference in how data is understood and acted upon. In addition, creativity in data science often involves exploring unconventional methods, testing out new algorithms, or combining techniques from various disciplines. Data scientists who think creatively are more willing to experiment, take risks, and try out novel approaches. This ability to innovate is what drives progress in the field, leading to the development of new methodologies, tools, and technologies. Many of the most significant breakthroughs in data science—such as the rise of deep learning or the development of recommendation engines—came from individuals who were willing to think creatively, challenge traditional methods, and explore new possibilities. Ultimately, creativity in data science is not just about finding solutions but about pushing the boundaries of what's possible with data. It allows data scientists to see opportunities where others see obstacles and to turn raw data into insights that have a real-world impact. By embracing creativity alongside technical skills, data scientists can unlock new ways of thinking, bring fresh solutions to old problems, and continue driving innovation in the field.

Defining Creativity in Data Science

Creativity in data science doesn't always take the form of artistic expression, but it does involve thinking outside the box and using unconventional methods to solve problems. For a data scientist, creativity often means being able to look at a problem from different angles, envision alternative solutions, and apply techniques in unexpected ways. It involves combining technical knowledge with an innovative mindset to overcome challenges that cannot be solved by standard procedures or tools. Many problems in data science are open-ended, and often, the data scientist has to figure out not only how to answer the questions being asked but also what questions are worth asking in the first place. This requires a creative approach—one that allows for ambiguity, experimentation, and trial-and-error. While creativity might seem at odds with the structured, analytical nature of data science, it's actually the driving force behind some of the most impactful breakthroughs in the field.

The Need for Creativity in Problem Solving

One of the keyways that creativity manifests in data science is in problem-solving. Real-world data is rarely clean or complete, and data scientists are often tasked with making sense of messy, unstructured, or incomplete datasets. Standard approaches don't always work in these situations. This is where creativity comes into play—allowing data scientists to think outside conventional boundaries and find ways to fill in the gaps, reframe the problem, or experiment with alternative methods. Imagine you're working on a predictive model for customer churn, but the dataset has significant gaps in customer interaction history. A straightforward approach might involve ignoring the missing data, but a creative data scientist will think more deeply about how to handle this challenge. They might look for external data sources to augment the existing data, use innovative data imputation methods to fill in the blanks or devise a model that accounts for missing information by weighting certain variables differently. Each of these solutions requires creativity to overcome the limitations of the data. Creativity also plays a crucial role in feature engineering, the process of selecting, modifying, and creating new variables (features) from raw data to improve model performance. Often, the best-performing models are not those with the most advanced algorithms but those that use creatively engineered features to capture meaningful patterns in the data. A data scientist might, for example, create new features based on domain knowledge, transform time-based data into seasonal trends, or design features that represent complex relationships between variables.

Creative Approaches to Data Visualization

Another area where creativity is essential is in data visualization. While data visualization tools like charts, graphs, and dashboards are common, the most effective visualizations require more than just technical proficiency with these tools. They require creative thinking to present complex data in a way that is clear, engaging, and meaningful to the intended audience. A well-designed visualization can transform a complicated dataset into a compelling narrative, allowing stakeholders to understand the data's implications at a glance. This often requires creative approaches to storytelling through data. Rather than simply presenting the data as a static chart, a data scientist might use interactive dashboards, creative visual metaphors, or dynamic visuals that highlight key trends over time. For example, a traditional bar chart might show sales trends over a year, but a creative data scientist could enhance this by creating an interactive visualization that allows users to explore sales by region, product category, and customer segment. Alternatively, they might use a storytelling approach, building a series of visualizations that walk the audience through the factors driving sales fluctuations, using color, size, and animation to emphasize the most important insights. These creative approaches not only make the data more accessible but also help decision-makers engage with and act upon the insights. Creativity in data visualization is especially important when the data is complex or when the audience has limited technical knowledge. In these cases, creative visualization can bridge the gap between technical analysis and practical decision-making by translating the data into a form that is easy to understand and interpret.

Innovating with New Tools and Techniques

The field of data science is constantly evolving, with new tools, algorithms, and methodologies emerging at a rapid pace. Creativity is essential for data scientists to stay ahead of the curve, adapt to these changes, and experiment with new techniques. This might mean trying out a new machine learning algorithm, experimenting with unsupervised learning techniques, or exploring a novel data processing framework. Innovation in data science is often driven by curiosity combined with creativity. When faced with a problem that traditional methods can't solve, a creative data scientist is willing to take risks and try something new. This might involve adapting algorithms from other fields, combining multiple techniques to create a hybrid solution, or inventing entirely new ways to process data. Take the rise of deep learning, for example. The development of neural networks and other deep learning models was a creative leap forward in data science. Instead of relying on traditional statistical models, researchers and data scientists explored how to model the human brain's learning processes, applying that understanding to develop systems that can recognize patterns in data with unprecedented accuracy. Creativity is at the heart of this type of innovation, as it requires data scientists to think beyond existing paradigms and explore new possibilities.

Creativity in Collaboration and Communication

Creativity also extends to how data scientists collaborate with others and communicate their findings. Often, data scientists work with teams of people from different disciplines, business leaders, engineers, marketers, and developers. These stakeholders may have little to no background in data science, so effectively communicating insights to them requires creativity. A creative data scientist finds ways to make complex concepts and technical details accessible to non-experts. This might involve crafting analogies, designing interactive reports, or finding creative ways to highlight the most important information without overwhelming the audience with data. The ability to creatively communicate findings can make the difference between a data-driven insight being implemented or ignored. Collaboration in data science is also an area where creativity shines. When working with diverse teams, creative thinking helps bridge the gap between different areas of expertise. A data scientist who can think creatively about how to integrate data science solutions into business processes or product development is invaluable. This collaborative creativity is what leads to the development of innovative products, services, and strategies that have real-world impact.

The Balance Between Creativity and Structure

While creativity is a vital aspect of data science, it must be balanced with the structured, analytical nature of the field. Creativity without rigor can lead to unfounded conclusions or inefficient methods, while structure without creativity can lead to missed opportunities and stagnant approaches. The most effective data scientists know how to strike a balance between the two. Creativity allows data scientists to explore new possibilities, but critical thinking helps them evaluate the viability of those possibilities. In practice, this means approaching creative solutions with a skeptical mind—testing, validating, and refining ideas until they are both innovative and reliable. This balance ensures that the creative leaps taken in data science are grounded in evidence and aligned with the goals of the project. For example, when experimenting with a new feature engineering technique, a data scientist might first brainstorm multiple ways to transform the data creatively. But once those ideas are on the table, they must rigorously test each one to see if it truly improves the model's performance. This iterative process of creativity followed by evaluation is what drives progress in data science. Creativity in data science is about more than just algorithms or models—it's about approaching problems with an open mind, looking for new ways to use data, and communicating insights in a compelling and impactful way. Whether it's devising new solutions to complex problems, visualizing data in a way that tells a story, or experimenting with the latest tools and techniques, creativity is essential to the data science process. As we continue through the book, we'll explore how creativity interacts with critical thinking and curiosity to form a holistic approach to data science that not only solves problems but also pushes the boundaries of what's possible. By embracing creativity alongside the technical and analytical aspects of the field, data scientists can unlock new opportunities for discovery and innovation.

CHAPTER 5

BLENDING CREATIVITY AND CRITICAL THINKING IN PROBLEM SOLVING

Data science exists at the fascinating crossroads of art and science, where the structured logic of analysis meets the boundless possibilities of innovation. In this space, solutions are often created by combining seemingly opposing forces: creativity and critical thinking. These two skills, at first glance, may seem like they reside on opposite ends of the spectrum. Creativity encourages expansive thinking, generating new ideas, exploring possibilities, and imagining what could be. It is the source of innovation, allowing data scientists to ask unconventional questions and think outside traditional boundaries. On the other hand, critical thinking focuses on precision, evaluation, and discernment. It involves questioning assumptions, applying logic, and ensuring that decisions are backed by evidence and sound reasoning. In the world of data science, these two skills are not only compatible, but they are also essential to one another. Creativity without critical thinking can result in ideas that are imaginative but impractical or unsupported by data. Critical thinking without creativity, on the other hand, can lead to a rigid, formulaic approach that misses new opportunities or innovative solutions. The most effective data scientists understand that true problem-solving occurs when these two traits are used in tandem. Creativity allows them to explore novel ideas and push the boundaries of what is possible, while critical thinking ensures that those ideas are refined, tested, and grounded in reality. This chapter delves into the symbiotic relationship between creativity and critical thinking in data science. We will explore how these skills interact at every stage of the data science process, from problem definition to data exploration, model building, and communication. By blending creativity and critical thinking, data scientists can arrive at innovative, impactful solutions that are not only imaginative but also actionable and reliable.

The Complementary Nature of Creativity and Critical Thinking

At first glance, creativity and critical thinking might seem like opposing forces. Creativity is often associated with divergent thinking, exploring new ideas, pushing boundaries, and imagining what could be. It is the process that encourages free thinking, innovation, and the generation of multiple solutions to a problem. In contrast, critical thinking is more about convergent thinking, narrowing down ideas, testing assumptions, and applying logic to determine the best course of action. It is a more structured process, focused on evaluation, analysis, and evidence-based decision-making. However, in data science, these two modes of thinking are not only compatible but essential to each other. Creativity without critical thinking can lead to impractical or unfeasible solutions, while critical thinking without creativity can result in a rigid, unimaginative approach that fails to take advantage of new possibilities. Together, creativity and critical thinking form a powerful combination that allows data scientists to explore a wide range of ideas while ensuring that the final solution is grounded in reality and backed by evidence.

Creativity and Critical Thinking in Problem Definition

The first step in any data science project is defining the problem, and this is where creativity and critical thinking must begin to work in tandem. When a data scientist is presented with a business challenge or a research question, the first task is to clarify what exactly needs to be solved. This is not always straightforward, as problems in data science are often complex and multi-faceted. A creative data scientist will begin by thinking broadly, exploring all possible interpretations of the problem and considering different angles. For example, a company might ask, "How can we reduce customer churn?" On the surface, this seems like a simple question, but a creative approach would explore multiple dimensions of churn—such as identifying customer segments at the highest risk, understanding the root causes of churn, or predicting when churn is most likely to happen. Creativity allows the data scientist to frame the problem in a way that opens up new possibilities for analysis. Once creative exploration has generated a range of potential questions, critical thinking comes into play. The data scientist must now evaluate these different interpretations of the problem, determining which ones are feasible given the available data and business constraints. Critical thinking helps the data scientist prioritize questions, focusing on those that are most actionable and relevant to the organization's goals. This process of narrowing down creative ideas ensures that the final problem definition is both innovative and realistic.

Exploring Data with Creativity, Evaluating with Critical Thinking

When the problem has been clearly defined, the next step is to explore the data. This is one of the most exciting and creative parts of data science because it involves uncovering patterns, relationships, and trends that may not be immediately obvious. A creative data scientist approaches data exploration with curiosity and an open mind, looking beyond the standard variables and metrics to discover hidden insights. For instance, in a project aimed at improving customer retention, a data scientist might go beyond traditional customer behavior data and explore less obvious factors such as website interaction patterns, customer support call frequency, or even social media engagement. Creativity in data exploration often involves asking unconventional questions, such as, "What data points are we overlooking?" or "How might these different variables interact in ways we haven't considered?" However, creative exploration must be tempered with critical thinking to ensure that the patterns found in the data are meaningful and not just coincidental. After identifying potential insights, a data scientist needs to rigorously test their validity. This is where critical thinking becomes essential evaluating whether the patterns hold up under different conditions, ensuring that they are not the result of random noise, and considering alternative explanations. For example, a correlation between increased customer service calls and churn might seem significant, but a critical thinker will question whether this is a causal relationship or if both factors are influenced by a third variable, such as product dissatisfaction. By blending creativity with critical thinking in data exploration, data scientists can generate new insights while ensuring that those insights are accurate, reliable, and actionable.

Creative Model Building and Critical Model Evaluation

One of the key technical tasks of a data scientist is building predictive models, and creativity plays an important role in this process. Creative model building involves thinking about which features (variables) to include, how to transform the data, and which algorithms to use. It also requires experimentation—trying different approaches to see which works best. A creative data scientist might experiment with feature engineering, combining multiple variables to create new ones that capture more complex relationships in the data. They might also try novel algorithms or hybrid models that blend multiple techniques to achieve better results. But as with data exploration, creativity in model building must be balanced with critical thinking. Once a model has been built, critical evaluation is crucial to ensure that it performs well and generalizes new data. This means assessing the model's accuracy, testing it on different datasets, and looking for signs of overfitting or underfitting. A critical thinker will also consider the interpretability of the model—ensuring that the model is not only accurate but also understandable and transparent to stakeholders. Critical thinking in model evaluation goes beyond just looking at performance metrics like accuracy or precision. It involves questioning the assumptions underlying the model, understanding its limitations, and considering its ethical implications. For example, a highly accurate model that is difficult to interpret may not be useful in certain contexts, such as in healthcare or finance, where transparency and explainability are critical. A creative solution combined with critical evaluation ensures that the model is not only innovative but also practical and aligned with the needs of the organization.

Balancing Creativity and Critical Thinking in Communication

The final stage of any data science project is communicating the results to stakeholders, and here again, creativity and critical thinking must work together. Creativity is essential for finding ways to present complex data and insights in a way that is engaging and easy to understand. This might involve creating interactive dashboards, using storytelling techniques to guide stakeholders through the findings, or designing visualizations that highlight the most important trends. However, while creativity helps make the insights more accessible, critical thinking ensures that the communication is accurate, clear, and actionable. A data scientist must critically evaluate the message they are conveying, making sure that the insights are presented honestly and transparently, without oversimplification or exaggeration. Critical thinking also helps the data scientist anticipate potential questions or concerns from stakeholders, ensuring that they are prepared to explain the limitations of the analysis and address any uncertainties. In the field of data science, creativity and critical thinking are not opposing forces—they are complementary skills that, when combined, lead to more effective problem-solving. Creativity allows data scientists to explore new ideas, ask unconventional questions, and generate innovative solutions, while critical thinking ensures that those solutions are grounded in evidence, logic, and practicality. Together, these two skills form the foundation of effective data science, enabling data scientists to tackle complex problems with both imagination and rigor. As we move forward, we'll continue to explore how this dynamic interaction between creativity and critical thinking can drive impactful results in data science.

CHAPTER 6

ASKING THE RIGHT QUESTIONS: THE CORE OF DATA SCIENCE

At the heart of every successful data science project lies the ability to ask the right questions. The quality of the questions you ask directly influences the depth and value of the insights you uncover. Data science is not merely about running algorithms or crunching numbers; it's about solving real-world problems through data, and this journey starts with asking the right questions. These questions guide your exploration, shape your analysis, and ultimately determine whether your findings will be meaningful, actionable, and impactful. Without the right questions, even the most advanced data techniques can lead you astray or provide superficial insights that don't address the core issue. The process of asking the right questions in data science is far from trivial. Often, the problems presented at the outset are broad, ambiguous, or not fully understood. It's the job of the data scientist to refine these initial questions, breaking them down into more focused, answerable components that direct the analysis in a purposeful way. For example, a business might come to a data team with the question, **"How can we improve our sales?"** While this question is a good starting point, it's too vague to be actionable.

A skilled data scientist will ask more precise follow-up questions like, **"Which customer segments are contributing the most to sales growth?"** or **"What product categories are performing best across different demographics?"** By refining the initial question, the data scientist turns a broad problem into a more manageable and data-driven inquiry. This ability to ask insightful, focused questions is not just a product of technical knowledge; it is driven by curiosity and critical thinking. Curiosity fuels the desire to dig deeper into the data, pushing the data scientist to explore different dimensions of the problem. It encourages them to ask not just "What happened?" but also **"Why did it happen?"** and **"What could happen next?"** Curiosity leads to the discovery of hidden patterns, unexpected correlations, and new angles that can bring fresh insights. On the other hand, critical thinking plays a vital role in ensuring that the questions being asked are both relevant and rigorous. It helps the data scientist evaluate whether the questions are truly addressing the heart of the problem, whether they are based on sound assumptions, and whether they can be answered with the available data. Critical thinking also keeps the data scientist focused, preventing them from chasing irrelevant questions or getting distracted by interesting but ultimately insignificant trends in the data. In this chapter, we will explore why asking the right questions is the foundation of effective data science. We will examine the interplay between curiosity and critical thinking in the process of framing questions and see how this step shapes every aspect of the data science workflow. Ultimately, the questions you ask determine the direction of your analysis and the value of the insights you deliver, making them one of the most important tools in the data scientist's toolkit.

The Importance of Problem Framing

Every data science project starts with a problem. Whether you're working for a business looking to improve sales, a healthcare organization aiming to improve patient outcomes, or a government agency trying to optimize resource allocation, the process begins with a need or a challenge that data can help address. However, these problems are often vague or poorly defined, and part of a data scientist's role is to frame the problem in a way that is clear and solvable. For example, a company might come to you with a broad request: **"How can we increase revenue?"** While this is a valid question, it's too broad and doesn't provide enough focus for a meaningful data science approach. A better-framed question could be: **"What customer segments show the most potential for increased spending, and what factors drive their purchasing decisions?"** This refined question gives the data scientist a clear direction, highlighting which areas to explore and what kinds of data will be useful. Framing the right problem involves creativity to think about the issue from different perspectives, curiosity to explore the underlying causes, and critical thinking to narrow down the scope into something measurable and actionable.

Exploring Different Types of Questions

In data science, questions can take many forms, but they generally fall into three broad categories: descriptive, predictive, and prescriptive. Each type of question serves a different purpose and requires a different approach.

Descriptive questions ask, "What happened?" These are the most basic questions and involve exploring historical data to understand past trends or behaviors. For example, "What were our sales figures last quarter?" or "Which products had the highest return rates?"

Predictive questions ask, "What will happen?" These questions build on historical data and apply models to forecast future events. For instance, "Which customers are likely to churn in the next three months?" or "How will demand for our products fluctuate next year?"

Prescriptive questions ask, "What should we do?" These are the most advanced questions and involve recommending actions based on the data. For example, "What marketing strategy should we implement to reduce customer churn?" or "How should we adjust inventory levels to optimize supply chain efficiency?"

The ability to recognize which type of question to ask is critical to solving the problem at hand. Starting with a descriptive question can help establish the context, while predictive questions move toward actionable insights. Prescriptive questions offer concrete recommendations, ensuring that the data-driven insights lead to effective decision-making.

Using Curiosity to Uncover Deeper Insights

Curiosity plays a central role in helping data scientists ask better questions. It drives you to dig deeper, challenge assumptions, and continuously refine your approach. Rather than simply accepting data at face value, a curious data scientist constantly asks follow-up questions: **"Why is this happening?" "What's driving this trend?" "What patterns am I** missing?" This habit of continuous inquiry opens the door to more meaningful and insightful analysis. For example, imagine you are analyzing customer churn for an e-commerce company. Your initial question might be, **"Which customers are likely to churn?"** But as you dive into the data, curiosity pushes you to ask further questions: **"Why do certain customers churn more than others?"** or **"Are there any specific actions customers take before they stop using our service?"** These follow-up questions help you move from simply predicting churn to uncovering the root causes, which in turn leads to more actionable insights. Curiosity also encourages experimentation. A curious data scientist isn't afraid to test multiple hypotheses, explore different datasets, or experiment with new algorithms. This willingness to explore increases the likelihood of discovering hidden patterns and correlations that can significantly impact decision-making.

Critical Thinking in Question Refinement

While curiosity opens the door to exploration, critical thinking ensures that you stay focused on asking the most relevant and actionable questions. Critical thinking helps you evaluate the validity and relevance of each question, ensuring that you aren't chasing insights that are interesting but ultimately irrelevant to solving the core problem. For instance, during the data exploration phase, it's easy to get sidetracked by interesting trends that might not actually matter. You might notice a curious spike in sales during a particular week and start digging into possible causes. However, a critical thinker will step back and ask, **"Is this spike significant in the context of our larger goal, or is it just an anomaly?"** Critical thinking helps you filter out distractions and focus on questions that will drive meaningful insights. Additionally, critical thinking helps refine your questions to make them more precise and measurable. For example, a question like, **"Why are customers leaving our service?"** can be too broad to answer effectively. A critical thinker will refine this to something like, **"What are the most common behaviors of customers who cancel their subscriptions within the first three months?"** This refined question is easier to answer with data and provides a clear direction for the analysis.

The Iterative Process of Questioning

Asking the right questions is not a one-time event. It's an iterative process that evolves as you gain more insights from the data. A data science project rarely follows a straight line from problem to solution. Instead, it involves cycles of questioning, analysis, and refinement. As new information comes to light, the questions evolve, becoming more focused and actionable. For instance, you might start with a broad question like, **"What factors influence customer churn?"** As you explore the data, you might discover that customer engagement is a key factor. This leads to a new, more focused question: **"Which specific engagement behaviors are most strongly correlated with churn?"** From there, further analysis might reveal that customers who don't interact with customer service are more likely to churn, prompting yet another question: **"How can we increase customer service interactions for at-risk customers?"** This iterative approach ensures that you are constantly refining your understanding of the problem and moving closer to a solution. It also highlights the importance of flexibility in data science. A good data scientist is always open to changing their approach based on new insights, adapting their questions to get the most value from the data. In data science, asking the right questions is arguably the most critical part of the process. The quality of your questions determines the quality of your insights, and the ability to continuously refine those questions is key to finding meaningful, actionable solutions. By blending curiosity with critical thinking, data scientists can ensure that they are not only exploring the data deeply but also focusing on questions that will lead to real-world impact.

LATEEF OKUNADE

CHAPTER 7

THE ART OF DATA STORYTELLING

Data science is often associated with technical expertise—coding, algorithms, and statistical analysis. However, while these technical skills are essential, one of the most overlooked yet crucial aspects of data science is the ability to communicate complex insights in a way that others can easily understand and act upon. This is where the art of data storytelling comes into play. Data storytelling is the process of transforming raw data into a compelling narrative that not only conveys insights but also inspires action. It goes beyond presenting numbers, graphs, or even sophisticated algorithms. Effective data storytelling requires the ability to weave a narrative around the data, making it meaningful, relatable, and relevant to the audience. At its core, data storytelling is about bridging the gap between technical data analysis and actionable business or operational decisions.

Regardless of how advanced or insightful the analysis is, if the findings cannot be communicated effectively, they may fail to make an impact. Data storytelling ensures that the audience—whether they are business executives, clients, or technical teams—can fully grasp the significance of the insights and, more importantly, take appropriate action based on those insights. This storytelling process involves more than just visualizing data through charts or graphs. It requires a deep understanding of the problem at hand, the audience's needs, and the narrative that will resonate with them. A well-crafted story can contextualize the data, showing not only what the data says but also why it matters. In this chapter, we will explore the critical role of data storytelling in data science, examining how creativity and critical thinking are essential tools in enhancing storytelling. We'll also discuss how a well-structured narrative can elevate your data work, making it not just insightful but also highly impactful for decision-making.

Why Data Storytelling Matters

At its core, data storytelling is about communication. No matter how advanced the analysis or how powerful the model, insights are only valuable if they are communicated effectively. Stakeholders, decision-makers, or clients may not have a deep understanding of data science, and it is up to the data scientist to bridge that gap. Data storytelling turns complex analyses into clear, engaging narratives that can drive decision-making. For example, imagine you've built a model predicting customer churn with 95% accuracy. While this is a technically impressive result, simply presenting this figure to a non-technical stakeholder may not lead to action. The number alone doesn't explain what factors drive churn, how the prediction was made, or what should be done next. Data storytelling involves creating a narrative around that 95%—explaining which customer behaviors are most predictive of churn, presenting this information visually, and suggesting actionable steps the business can take to retain those customers. By weaving a story around the data, you turn a technical achievement into a clear, actionable insight.

The Key Elements of Data Storytelling

Effective data storytelling is built around three key elements: data, visuals, and narrative. Each of these elements plays a crucial role in making the insights meaningful, engaging, and understandable.

Data: The foundation of any data story is, of course, the data itself. The insights drawn from your analysis should be accurate, relevant, and aligned with the problem at hand. Critical thinking ensures that the data is clean, reliable, and valid before it becomes the basis of the story. Without accurate data, even the best story falls apart.

Visuals: Visuals are a powerful tool for making complex data easier to understand. Creative data scientists use charts, graphs, and interactive dashboards to highlight key insights and make the data more accessible. Visuals are particularly effective because they help the audience quickly grasp trends, comparisons, and outliers that might otherwise be hidden in the raw data. However, it's important to use visuals wisely over complex or poorly designed charts can confuse rather than clarify. Creativity is key here: finding the right visual representation for your data is part of crafting a compelling story.

Narrative: The narrative is what ties the data and visuals together into a coherent story. It provides context, explains the significance of the findings, and guides the audience through the insights step by step. Without a strong narrative, the audience may not understand why the data matters or how to act on it. A good data narrative answers the question, "So what?" It highlights not just what the data says but also why it's important and what the next steps should be.

Crafting a Compelling Narrative

The art of storytelling is not just about conveying facts; it's about engaging the audience emotionally and intellectually. Even in data science, where numbers and logic dominate, storytelling plays a crucial role in making the insights resonate. Crafting a compelling narrative requires you to understand your audience, define your key message, and structure your story effectively.

Know your audience: Different audiences will require different levels of detail and focus. Executives might want a high-level overview of the insights and the implications for business strategy, while a technical team might want to dive deeper into the methodology and technical details. Understanding your audience allows you to tailor the narrative to their needs, ensuring that the story you tell is relevant and engaging to them.

Define your key message: Every data story should have a central message—a takeaway that you want your audience to remember. This message should be clear and concise, and all parts of the story should support it. For instance, if your key message is that customer churn is primarily driven by lack of engagement, every chart, graph, and explanation should be tied back to that point. A scattered or unfocused narrative can leave the audience confused and unsure of what to take away from the data.

Structure your story: A good data story has a clear structure, much like any other narrative. Start with the context, what problem or question are you trying to solve? Then move on to the insights—what does the data reveal? Finally, end with the implications, what actions should be taken based on these insights? Structuring your story this way helps guide the audience through the data logically and ensures that they understand not just what the data says, but why it matters.

Blending Creativity and Critical Thinking in Storytelling

As with other aspects of data science, creativity and critical thinking both play essential roles in data storytelling. Creativity is key to finding engaging ways to present the data, whether through innovative visuals or compelling narratives. It's about thinking beyond the typical bar charts and line graphs, finding visual metaphors or interactive elements that make the data come alive for the audience. Creative storytelling can transform raw data into something that resonates with the audience, making the insights more memorable and actionable. However, creativity must be grounded in critical thinking. While it's tempting to create dramatic visuals or weave an emotionally engaging story, it's essential that the data and narrative remain accurate and trustworthy. Critical thinking ensures that the story is based on solid evidence, that the visuals are not misleading, and that the narrative doesn't overstate the significance of the findings. A balance between creativity and critical thinking is what makes data storytelling both compelling and credible.

Turning Insights into Action

The ultimate goal of data storytelling is not simply to inform but to inspire action. It is not enough to present data or highlight interesting patterns; the real impact of data science lies in guiding decision-makers toward concrete steps that can improve outcomes. A well-told data story goes beyond numbers and findings—it delivers a clear, actionable message that leads the audience to a decision or encourages them to take meaningful action. Whether you're presenting to business executives, policymakers, or a technical team, the story should always culminate in actionable recommendations. For instance, if a data story uncovers that customer churn is driven by poor customer service interactions, the narrative should end with clear suggestions: improving customer service training, increasing support staff, or deploying new customer engagement tools. Without these specific recommendations, the insights may seem interesting, but they will fail to drive real change. Data storytelling provides not only the "what" but also the "so what" and "now what." It moves the audience from understanding the issue to considering practical solutions. In a business context, this could involve proposing changes to the company's strategy or recommending operational adjustments based on the data. In a research setting, it might suggest further areas for investigation or potential experimentation. In all cases, the goal is to provide clarity and direction, leaving the audience with a firm grasp of the insights and a concrete understanding of what should be done next. Ultimately, a good data story ensures that the audience is not only informed but also empowered to take decisive action. This is where data storytelling achieves its full potential—by transforming insights into meaningful outcomes that improve processes, strategies, or decision-making across an organization. Data storytelling is an essential skill in data science, transforming complex analyses into insights that people can understand, engage with, and act on. By blending creativity and critical thinking, data scientists can craft compelling narratives that communicate the true value of their work. As we continue, we'll explore how data scientists can tackle ambiguity and uncertainty in their work, and how curiosity plays a role in navigating those challenges.

LATEEF OKUNADE

CHAPTER 8

TACKLING AMBIGUITY: NAVIGATING UNCERTAINTY IN DATA

In the world of data science, ambiguity is inevitable. Whether it's dealing with incomplete datasets, conflicting information, or unpredictable variables, data scientists must frequently make sense of uncertainty and still move forward. Unlike other fields where decisions might be based on a complete set of facts, data science often operates in an environment where the data is messy, incomplete, or sometimes contradictory. This uncertainty is part of the job, and rather than viewing it as a hindrance, successful data scientists see ambiguity as an opportunity for exploration and innovation.

Tackling ambiguity requires a unique combination of skills, including curiosity, creativity, and critical thinking. These skills enable data scientists to navigate through uncertain situations, identify meaningful patterns within the noise, and ultimately make informed, data-driven decisions despite the lack of clarity. Curiosity pushes data scientists to ask the right questions and dig deeper, exploring different angles to find new perspectives in the data. Creativity allows them to think outside the box, generating innovative solutions to fill gaps or work around limitations. Meanwhile, critical thinking ensures that even in the face of ambiguity, data scientists evaluate their findings carefully, assess the reliability of their data sources, and make sound judgments based on the evidence at hand.

Navigating uncertainty is not just about solving the problem at hand; it's about being comfortable with experimentation, iteration, and learning from failure. As data scientists experiment with different models, test various hypotheses, and explore new datasets, they are often led to surprising insights that might not have been obvious at first glance. This process of trial and error can reveal hidden connections or patterns, leading to better problem-solving and, ultimately, more innovative solutions. Embracing ambiguity allows data scientists to remain flexible, adapt to changing circumstances, and push the boundaries of what's possible in their field.

Embracing Uncertainty as Part of the Process

Ambiguity can be frustrating, especially for those who prefer clear-cut answers. However, in data science, ambiguity is not only common—it's essential to the process of discovery. Many of the most valuable insights come from situations where the data is incomplete, messy, or contradictory. Rather than viewing uncertainty as a barrier, successful data scientists see it as an opportunity to explore, experiment, and learn. For example, a business might present a vague problem, such as "Why are sales decreasing?" There could be countless contributing factors, from changes in consumer behavior to competitive pressure or shifts in the market. Instead of becoming overwhelmed by the complexity, a data scientist must embrace the ambiguity, asking open-ended questions like "What unexpected factors could be influencing sales?" and "How can we test different hypotheses with the available data?" Ambiguity encourages creative problem-solving because it forces data scientists to think beyond the obvious. They must navigate uncertainty by exploring different angles, developing multiple hypotheses, and testing various models. This iterative process of experimentation is what leads to breakthroughs.

Critical Thinking in the Face of Uncertainty

While creativity helps data scientists generate potential solutions in the face of ambiguity, critical thinking is what ensures that these solutions are grounded in reality. Critical thinking helps data scientists evaluate which pieces of information are reliable, identify gaps in the data, and assess the limitations of the available data. For example, imagine you are analyzing customer feedback for a new product, but the feedback data is incomplete or skewed toward a particular group of customers. A critical thinker would ask, "What biases might exist in this dataset? Are there other data sources we can use to fill the gaps?" Rather than jumping to conclusions based on limited information, critical thinking enables the data scientist to critically assess the available data and consider what assumptions they are making. In these situations, critical thinking also plays a crucial role in decision-making. When data is incomplete or ambiguous, the data scientist must carefully evaluate the risks of making decisions based on limited information. This might involve creating scenarios or models to test different assumptions, assessing the trade-offs of each decision, and being transparent about the uncertainty involved in the recommendations.

Curiosity as the Driver for Exploration

Curiosity is what pushes data scientists to explore beyond the surface, especially when the data is ambiguous. In the face of uncertainty, a curious mindset leads to the generation of more questions rather than settling for incomplete answers. Instead of being satisfied with what's immediately visible in the data, a curious data scientist will dig deeper, asking, "What's missing here?" or "What else could explain this outcome?" When dealing with ambiguous data, curiosity encourages experimentation. It drives data scientists to explore unconventional data sources, try out different algorithms, or use innovative methods to fill in the gaps. For example, if a retail company lacks sufficient purchase history data for a subset of customers, a curious data scientist might explore using social media data or web browsing patterns to supplement the missing information. Curiosity also leads data scientists to question assumptions, ensuring they remain open to multiple possibilities rather than getting locked into a single explanation. This mindset is essential for navigating ambiguous data because it fosters an environment of continuous learning and flexibility.

Strategies for Managing Ambiguity

There are several strategies that data scientists use to manage ambiguity and navigate uncertainty in their work. These strategies are designed to help them make the best possible decisions, even when the data is incomplete or unclear.

Start with the best available data: Even if the data is incomplete, it's essential to start with what's available. Identify key variables that can help shape the initial analysis, and then use creative thinking to fill in gaps where necessary.

Iterate and experiment: When dealing with ambiguity, iterative approaches are key. Testing different hypotheses and models allows you to refine your analysis and explore alternative explanations for the data. Iteration helps reduce uncertainty by progressively narrowing down possibilities.

Cross-validate with other data sources: When facing gaps or inconsistencies in the data, look for additional data sources that can complement the primary dataset. For example, customer surveys might be combined with behavioral data from web analytics to provide a fuller picture.

Communicate uncertainty clearly: Data scientists must be transparent with stakeholders about the limitations of the data and the level of uncertainty in their analysis. Communicating uncertainty is essential for managing expectations and ensuring that decision-makers are fully informed before acting on the data.

Focus on what can be controlled: In ambiguous situations, it's crucial to focus on what can be measured and controlled. Even if some aspects of the data are unclear, actionable insights can often be derived from the areas where the data is reliable.

The Value of Ambiguity in Data Science

While ambiguity is often viewed as a challenge, it can also serve as a powerful catalyst for growth and innovation. In data science, ambiguity is not something to be feared or avoided—it's an opportunity for deeper exploration, creative problem-solving, and fresh discoveries. When faced with incomplete or uncertain data, data scientists are pushed to think outside the box, develop new methodologies, and experiment with unconventional approaches. This need to work through ambiguity can often lead to more innovative and effective solutions. Ambiguous data often forces data scientists to become resourceful, exploring alternative data sources or creating hybrid models to address gaps. For example, if traditional customer data is limited or insufficient, a data scientist might turn to external sources like social media behavior, weather patterns, or economic indicators to complement the analysis. This not only fills gaps but also broadens the perspective, offering richer, more holistic insights than might have been achieved with a single data source. In this way, ambiguity encourages data scientists to experiment with new combinations of data and methodologies, which can lead to unexpected and valuable results.

In the field of machine learning, models trained on imperfect or incomplete data often end up being more adaptable and robust. By confronting the limitations of the data head-on, data scientists can build models that perform well across a variety of contexts, handling the unexpected better than models trained on perfectly clean data. This is because the models have been exposed to uncertainty during training, making them more resilient and better able to generalize across different datasets and scenarios. Thus, ambiguity plays a vital role in fostering innovation. It pushes data scientists to look beyond the obvious, experiment with new techniques, and ultimately develop solutions that are more flexible, adaptable, and capable of handling real-world complexities. Ambiguity and uncertainty are inevitable parts of the data science process, but rather than being paralyzed by the unknown, data scientists thrive when they embrace it. By combining curiosity, creativity, and critical thinking, they are able to navigate uncertainty, make informed decisions, and discover insights that others might overlook. As we continue, we will explore how intuition and data work together, and how data scientists can balance these two forces to make better decisions.

LATEEF OKUNADE

CHAPTER 9

THE BALANCE OF INTUITION AND DATA

In the realm of data science, facts, figures, and algorithms often take center stage. Yet, there is another element that plays a crucial role in decision-making: intuition. While data science is, at its core, an evidence-based discipline, the human element—intuition—cannot be ignored. Often, the best data scientists are those who not only rely on their models, data, and algorithms but also tap into their experience, insights, and gut instincts to guide their decisions. Intuition, though less quantifiable than data, serves as a valuable tool, especially when the data is incomplete, unclear, or too complex to fully understand without context. So, how does intuition fit into a field dominated by data-driven processes? For many, it may seem counterintuitive to bring "gut feelings" into a discipline centered on empirical evidence, but intuition, when used appropriately, is not random or unstructured. In fact, it is often built on years of experience, pattern recognition, and deep familiarity with the nuances of data.

Intuition allows data scientists to navigate uncertainty and explore possibilities that the data itself might not immediately be revealed. For example, when analyzing vast datasets, a seasoned data scientist may intuitively sense which variables are likely to have the greatest impact, or what kind of patterns might emerge from the data, even before conducting a formal analysis. In some cases, intuition serves as a starting point in the decision-making process. It can guide a data scientist's initial exploration of a dataset, helping them form hypotheses or narrow down the focus areas. This intuition isn't formed in isolation; it's rooted in prior experiences, a deep understanding of the subject matter, and familiarity with the data science methods that have worked in the past. When used correctly, intuition can serve as a compass, pointing toward the most promising avenues for further investigation.

However, the reliance on intuition must be carefully balanced with data-driven validation. While intuition provides direction, it must always be tested and validated against the evidence. The data scientist's role is to use critical thinking to assess whether their instincts align with the facts presented by the data. This means continually questioning assumptions, testing hypotheses, and using data to verify or refute gut feelings. In this way, critical thinking serves as the bridge between intuition and data, ensuring that decisions are grounded in both evidence and insight. The balance between intuition and data-driven analysis can lead to more holistic decision-making. While data is crucial for uncovering patterns, making predictions, and optimizing models, intuition adds a layer of human judgment that enriches the overall process. By blending the strengths of both, data scientists can arrive at well-rounded decisions that account for both the tangible facts and the more subtle, contextual factors that data alone may not capture.

The Role of Intuition in Data Science

Intuition often emerges from experience and a deep understanding of patterns, contexts, and nuances that data alone might not capture. In data science, intuition can help guide initial exploration, shape hypotheses, and provide direction when the data is incomplete or unclear. For example, a data scientist working in marketing may have years of experience understanding customer behavior. Even before the data is analyzed, their intuition might tell them that certain trends are likely to emerge or that specific customer segments will behave in a particular way. This instinct is not random—it's built from years of experience and pattern recognition. Intuition can help data scientists form early hypotheses that guide the exploration of data and help prioritize the factors they believe will be most influential. Intuition also plays a role when working with ambiguous or incomplete data. When the data is noisy or unreliable, intuition can help a data scientist make sense of the puzzle, narrowing down the possible causes or patterns. It allows them to make educated guesses, which can then be tested and validated through rigorous analysis.

When to Trust Your Gut

While intuition is valuable, it must be applied with caution. The danger of over-relying on intuition is that it can lead to bias or incorrect assumptions. Human intuition is often shaped by personal experiences, emotions, or cognitive biases, which can skew judgment. For example, confirmation bias—where individuals favor information that confirms their existing beliefs—can cause a data scientist to see what they expect to see, rather than what the data is actually saying. The key to using intuition in data science is to treat it as a starting point, not an endpoint. Intuition should guide exploration and help form hypotheses, but those instincts must be validated by data. A good data scientist knows when to trust their gut and when to turn to the data for confirmation. This balance ensures that the final decisions are grounded in evidence, not just intuition.

The Interplay Between Intuition and Data

Intuition and data are not opposing forces. In fact, the two can complement each other and lead to better, more holistic decision-making. Intuition can provide a starting point—a sense of where to look, what questions to ask, and which patterns might emerge. Data, on the other hand, provides the evidence needed to support or refute those initial instincts. For example, imagine a data scientist working for an e-commerce company. Their intuition might suggest that customers are likely to churn due to a new competitor entering the market. This instinct, based on knowledge of industry trends, can guide the exploration of customer behavior data, leading the data scientist to examine how customer engagement has changed since the competitor launched. From there, data analysis can either confirm or challenge the initial hypothesis. If the data supports the intuition, the data scientist can move forward with confidence. If the data contradicts the intuition, it provides an opportunity to reassess and adjust the approach. In many cases, the interplay between intuition and data creates a feedback loop. Intuition guides initial exploration, data provides evidence, and that evidence further refines the data scientist's intuition. This process allows for continuous learning and adaptation, leading to more nuanced and effective problem-solving.

Critical Thinking as the Bridge Between Intuition and Data

Critical thinking is what bridges the gap between intuition and data. It ensures that while intuition can guide exploration, it is always subject to scrutiny and validation through data. A data scientist who employs critical thinking is able to separate useful instincts from cognitive biases, ensuring that decisions are made based on logic and evidence. For example, critical thinking allows data scientists to question their assumptions and test their intuitions rigorously. It encourages them to ask, "Is this conclusion based on data, or is it driven by my preconceptions?" By applying a critical lens, data scientists can challenge their own instincts, seek out contradictory data, and ensure that they are not simply confirming what they already believe. Critical thinking also helps when intuition leads in a different direction than the data. In such cases, a data scientist may need to re-evaluate their initial instincts or look deeper into the data to see if something has been missed. Sometimes, this deeper investigation can reveal hidden patterns that support the original intuition, or it might expose new insights that were not initially considered. By fostering a mindset that values both intuition and evidence, critical thinking ensures that decisions are robust, well-informed, and free from bias.

Striking the Right Balance

The most successful data scientists understand that neither intuition nor data alone is sufficient to consistently make the best decisions. Striking the right balance between the two is crucial to arriving at the most effective outcomes. Too much reliance on data, without considering the value of intuition, can lead to overly complex models that may miss the bigger picture. Data alone, especially when vast or incomplete, doesn't always provide clear answers. In these cases, over-analyzing can lead to results that are accurate in theory but disconnected from practical realities or the nuances of the problem. On the other hand, depending solely on intuition, without validating it through data, can result in decisions that are based on assumptions or biases rather than hard evidence. Even experienced data scientists are susceptible to cognitive biases like confirmation bias, where they may favor information that supports their initial gut feeling. Without data to challenge or confirm these instincts, such decisions could lead to misleading conclusions or suboptimal results. The key is to strike a balance between the two approaches.

Data scientists must remain open to both instinct and evidence, recognizing the value that each brings to the table. Intuition can serve as a compass, helping guide the initial exploration of data and pointing toward potential insights. It can help data scientists focus on areas that, based on experience, are most likely to yield meaningful results. However, these instincts must be continually tested and refined through data validation. By using intuition to guide exploration and data to challenge assumptions, data scientists can ensure that their final conclusions are grounded in both experience and empirical evidence. This balance allows data scientists to benefit from the insights gained through intuition while ensuring that their decisions are data-driven, reliable, and less prone to bias. In the field of data science, the balance between intuition and data is key to making effective decisions. While data provides the evidence needed for sound decision-making, intuition adds an important layer of insight that comes from experience, context, and pattern recognition. By combining the two, and by using critical thinking as the bridge between them, data scientists can arrive at more informed, reliable, and impactful decisions. As we move to the final chapter, we'll discuss how these elements—creativity, curiosity, critical thinking, and intuition—come together to form the holistic mindset of a successful data scientist.

LATEEF OKUNADE

CHAPTER 10

THE HOLISTIC DATA SCIENTIST: INTEGRATING CREATIVITY, CURIOSITY, CRITICAL THINKING, AND INTUITION

Throughout this book, we've explored the key traits that set great data scientists apart from the rest: creativity, curiosity, critical thinking, and intuition. These traits, when considered individually, are powerful on their own and each plays a significant role in shaping how data scientists approach problems, uncover insights, and make decisions. Creativity opens the door to innovation, curiosity fuels exploration, critical thinking ensures accuracy and rigor, and intuition brings experience-based judgment to the forefront. However, while each trait is essential in its own right, its true power emerges when they are combined into a holistic approach. The most successful data scientists aren't just technical experts or skilled analysts, they are dynamic, flexible problem solvers who integrate these qualities to tackle complex challenges, generate innovative solutions, and transform raw data into actionable insights that drive real-world impact. This holistic mindset is what differentiates exceptional data scientists from the rest. It is not enough to simply be proficient with algorithms, models, or technical tools.

Data science is about solving problems—problems that are often messy, ambiguous, and multifaceted. In these situations, the ability to combine creativity, curiosity, critical thinking, and intuition is what enables data scientists to see the bigger picture, make sense of incomplete or noisy data, and deliver insights that matter. It's the interplay between these traits that allows data scientists to not only analyze data but also generate ideas, test hypotheses rigorously, and communicate findings in ways that inspire action. Creativity is the force that allows data scientists to think outside the box and devise novel solutions. It drives them to explore unconventional approaches, experiment with different methods, and push the boundaries of what's possible with data. Creativity becomes especially important when dealing with messy or incomplete datasets, where standard approaches may fall short.

Data scientists who cultivate creativity are better equipped to navigate uncertainty because they can reframe problems, use alternative data sources, and apply unique perspectives to find solutions that others might overlook. Curiosity, on the other hand, is the driving force behind exploration. It pushes data scientists to ask the right questions, dig deeper, and constantly seek out new insights. Curiosity prevents data scientists from stopping at surface-level answers and encourages them to look for hidden patterns, unexpected trends, and root causes. In a field like data science, where the answers are not always obvious, curiosity fosters the willingness to explore uncharted territory, test new ideas, and continuously learn and adapt. This relentless pursuit of understanding is what leads to breakthroughs that others might miss. Critical thinking, meanwhile, brings structure and rigor to the process.

While creativity and curiosity open the door to exploration, critical thinking ensures that the insights generated are valid, reliable, and actionable. It's the discipline of questioning assumptions, testing hypotheses, and evaluating data objectively. Critical thinking enables data scientists to filter out noise, identify meaningful patterns, and ensure that their conclusions are based on evidence. Without critical thinking, even the most creative ideas or interesting insights could lead to incorrect or misleading conclusions. Finally, intuition serves as a valuable guide, especially when working with incomplete data or uncertain outcomes. Intuition allows data scientists to draw on their experience, recognizing patterns and trends that might not be immediately apparent in the data. While data science is grounded in facts and figures, intuition adds an important human element to the decision-making process. It enables data scientists to connect the dots between what the data says and what their real-world experience tells them, helping them to make decisions that are not only data-driven but also contextually relevant.

When combined, these four traits—creativity, curiosity, critical thinking, and intuition—create a well-rounded, adaptable, and impactful data scientist. This integrated approach enables data scientists to tackle even the most complex and ambiguous problems with confidence and insight. They are not just technicians working with algorithms; they are problem solvers who can navigate uncertainty, balance innovation with rigor, and ultimately, deliver insights that drive meaningful change. As we conclude this exploration, it's clear that the best data scientists are those who embrace a holistic approach. By integrating these key traits, data scientists can transcend the role of technicians and become dynamic, adaptable professionals who not only analyze data but also shape the future with their insights. As the field continues to evolve, the data scientists who thrive will be those who cultivate this balance of creativity, curiosity, critical thinking, and intuition—unlocking the true potential of data and driving progress in their organizations and industries.

Creativity: Solving Problems in New Ways

Creativity is what allows data scientists to push the boundaries of what's possible with data. As we've discussed, creativity helps data scientists explore unconventional approaches, experiment with different methods, and find novel solutions to difficult problems. It's especially important when dealing with messy or incomplete data, where standard techniques may not apply. Creativity empowers data scientists to see possibilities where others see limitations. For example, instead of following rigid methodologies, creative data scientists will think about how to approach problems from new angles, like using unconventional data sources or developing custom features that more effectively capture the relationships within the data. Moreover, creativity plays a key role in how insights are communicated. Crafting a compelling data story requires a creative blend of visuals, narratives, and data points, ensuring that stakeholders can grasp the findings easily and engage with the recommendations.

Curiosity: Fueling Exploration

Curiosity drives the constant search for better questions, deeper insights, and broader perspectives. In data science, it's curiosity that fuels exploration and discovery, pushing data scientists to ask "why" and "what if" at every turn. This trait ensures that data scientists don't stop at surface-level insights but dig deeper to uncover root causes and hidden patterns that can unlock new opportunities. For example, a curious data scientist might look beyond standard metrics to ask, "What patterns haven't we considered?" or "Is there another explanation for this trend?" Curiosity also drives experimentation, encouraging data scientists to test new ideas and approaches, even when the outcome is uncertain. This willingness to explore uncharted territory often leads to breakthroughs that others might miss. Curiosity also promotes continuous learning. In a rapidly evolving field like data science, where new tools, techniques, and technologies emerge constantly, a curious mindset ensures that data scientists stay on top of the latest developments and continually improve their skills.

Critical Thinking: Evaluating and Refining Solutions

While creativity and curiosity push data scientists to explore and experiment, critical thinking brings structure, discipline, and rigor to the process. Critical thinking is essential for evaluating whether insights are valid, testing assumptions, and refining solutions to ensure they're grounded in logic and evidence. Without critical thinking, creative ideas and intuitive insights could lead to misleading conclusions or unreliable models. Critical thinking helps data scientists sift through the noise to identify meaningful patterns and actionable insights. For instance, after developing a creative solution or uncovering an unexpected pattern, critical thinking allows the data scientist to rigorously test the findings, ensuring they hold up under scrutiny. It involves asking, "Is this result valid? What biases might exist in the data? What alternative explanations should we consider?" Additionally, critical thinking ensures that data stories are not just compelling but accurate. It helps data scientists strike a balance between storytelling and precision, making sure that the narrative remains clear and actionable while also being truthful and evidence based.

Intuition: Making the Human Connection

Intuition, as we explored in the previous chapter, is the subtle but important force that connects the data to real-world experience. While data analysis is grounded in facts, intuition allows data scientists to draw on their experience, pattern recognition, and contextual knowledge to guide their decision-making. It serves as a valuable tool when dealing with incomplete data, uncertain outcomes, or highly complex problems. Intuition is particularly useful in the early stages of analysis when hypotheses are being formed and exploration is just beginning. A seasoned data scientist's gut feeling about which areas to focus on can significantly accelerate the analytical process. However, intuition must always be tempered by critical thinking and tested against the data to ensure that it's not biased or unfounded.

The Power of Integration: Combining All Four Traits

The true strength of a data scientist emerges when all these traits are combined into a holistic mindset. Individually, creativity, curiosity, critical thinking, and intuition each contribute to solving specific challenges. But when integrated, they create a dynamic, adaptable approach to problem-solving that enables data scientists to tackle even the most complex and ambiguous problems with confidence and insight.

Creativity generates new possibilities.

Curiosity drives exploration.

Critical thinking ensures rigor and discipline.

Intuition brings context and human insight.

Together, these traits help data scientists navigate the entire data science process—from framing the right questions, exploring the data, building models, and validating solutions to communicating insights effectively.

Adapting to an Ever-Changing Field

One of the most important aspects of this holistic approach is its adaptability. Data science is a constantly evolving field, and data scientists must continuously adapt to new tools, methods, and challenges. A data scientist who embodies creativity, curiosity, critical thinking, and intuition is well-positioned to thrive in this dynamic environment. Whether they're developing solutions for emerging technologies like artificial intelligence or navigating complex, unstructured data sources, this integrated mindset allows them to remain flexible and innovative, even in the face of uncertainty. In practice, this means being open to new ways of thinking, continually refining one's skills, and balancing creative exploration with disciplined analysis. It's about seeing the bigger picture while staying rooted in the details, allowing for a comprehensive and effective approach to data science. Becoming a successful data scientist is not just about mastering technical skills or memorizing algorithms. It's about cultivating a mindset that integrates creativity, curiosity, critical thinking, and intuition.

This holistic approach allows data scientists to navigate ambiguity, explore new ideas, test hypotheses rigorously, and, ultimately, deliver insights that make a real impact. By harnessing the power of these four traits, data scientists can transcend the role of a technician and become true problem solvers—people who not only analyze data but also shape the future with the insights they uncover. As the field of data science continues to evolve, the data scientists who thrive will be those who approach their work with a balance of logic and imagination, analysis and intuition. In this way, the most valuable tool in a data scientist's toolkit is not just their knowledge of algorithms or models, their ability to think holistically and embrace the full spectrum of skills needed to unlock the power of data.

www.ingramcontent.com/pod-product-compliance
Lightning Source LLC
LaVergne TN
LVHW091536070526
838199LV00001B/87